Childless

Childless
A collection of personal essays written by women without children

Essays by:
(writers in alphabetical order)

Hilary Crahan
Stephana de la Torre
Kiyomi Emi
Susan Hodges
Karen Kaye
Katherine Kolander
Lauren Lee
Liz Lundy
Maerice Simpson
Leisa B Vander Velde
Nancy Vick
Renea Washington
Shelley Wilson

Please note: Some of our writers wish to remain anonymous.

The essays are not in alphabetical order.

Copyright © 2010 by Hilary Crahan

All rights reserved. No part of this book may be reproduced, stored, or transmitted by any means—whether auditory, graphic, mechanical, or electronic—without written permission of both publisher and author, except in the case of brief excerpts used in critical articles and reviews. Unauthorized reproduction of any part of this work is illegal and is punishable by law.

ISBN 978-0-557-33292-2

Contents

Essay 1	1
Essay 2	7
Essay 3 Childless, or is it Childfree?	13
Essay 4 My Triangle	19
Essay 5	25
Essay 6	29
Essay 7 Child-Less or Child-Free?	33
Essay 8	37
Essay 9	41
Essay 10	45
Essay 11	49
Essay 12 Does Being 'Childless' Mean Being 'Without'?	53
Essay 13	59
Essay 14	63
Essay 15 Childless in a World of Kids	69
Essay 16	73

A friend told me people write words on paper when they feel passion for something. This book is a passion-project devoted to helping women know they are whole.

Whole, with or without children.

Whole, whether you wanted children, were ambivalent about having them, or definitely did not see yourself as a mother.

Whole and complete, without being marginalized or feeling alone.

It is not easy to face this topic, let alone talk about it. We, as women, don't discuss childlessness amongst ourselves. It isn't comfortable. Nonetheless, we persevere in making meaning of our experience.

In the privacy of our own hearts, we realize we are whole and complete just as we are.

To share how we arrive at this truth is to participate in a rite of passage that honors us all.

This book is written for those seeking freedom from a socially constructed identity, which says that women have babies.

As I navigated my personal journey, I longed for the light and love of female voices such as those contained herein. Hence was birthed the inspiration to put this collective wisdom in the hands of all women seeking other women's support.

Our compassion is the true passion that created Childless.

We, as women, are here to help and support one another. We are here to listen, guide, laugh, and cry. Together.

"Nothing in life is to be feared. It is only to be understood."
Marie Curie

The women in this book freely share their stories with you.
I am so grateful they said, "yes," to nurturing this project.

Please— a poem

please
    be patient and gentle
    with yourself

understanding life
    is
    a slow unfolding

and

you are simply
    in the midst of your own

becoming

please
    be patient and gentle
    with yourself

Hilary Crahan February 2010

"Choose to be happy. It is a way of being wise."
Collette

The intention of this book is to gather individual women's voices on the subject of being childless and to share this labor of love with you.

We hope our essays speak to you in a way that illuminates, soothes, and inspires. The only request we asked of our authors was that they be completely honest.

As you read our essays, you will hear grace, anger, humor, fear, fearlessness, forgiveness, confusion, joy, and acceptance.

"Childless" has been a life passage and a life lesson for each of us.

We created this tapestry of experience with care and love for each of you.

"With so many spectacular colors in the world, it's a shame to make everything black and white."
Dennis R. Little

❦ Essay 1 ☙

Being a single woman in her forties and childless, how does it feel? Where to start…I was brought up to believe being a wife and mother would lead to the most fulfilling life. I don't mean this to sound old-fashioned. Emphasis was also placed on a career, but the unspoken, innately known truth was motherhood trumped all. I would grow up, get married, and have kids. It all seemed so elementary – like breathing. I never questioned it. Just assumed it would happen. And desperately wanted it to happen.

But then I never met 'the one'. People kept saying, "Be patient, the right one will come along when you least expect it." Well, I'm still waiting. I played by the rules. Did everything I was supposed to. Or what I thought I was supposed to do. And time kept marching on. Until one day I realized the window was closed. How did this happen? How did I miss the boat? It snuck up on me. As if the decision got made for me. Such profound, far reaching consequences for an 'indecision'. It sounds dumb, I know, but that is how it unfolded. It was not that I met the right man and would not climb down off the corporate ladder. Quite the contrary…I did not meet 'the one'. Period.

I was angry, I was bitter, and I was mad. But most of all, I was palpably sad and empty. Why not me? It happens for every other woman. Rich or poor, big or small – from whatever walk of life, they all have kids. How can THEY have children and I don't? It shattered my self-image.

Where do you go from here? Well, you look for fulfillment in other areas – career being the obvious choice. So you work hard and give too much to a job. Yes, it has its gratifying moments, but it lacks the connectedness I longed for. Then what happens – you get severely misjudged and perceived as someone you are not. In fact, as someone you would never want to be. A cold career woman, who does not want to give up a self-centered life. I would have been delighted to do just that. What could be more fulfilling than creating and nurturing another life? But instead I am pegged as tough and unloving. Not at all who I am. And it's hurtful to be perceived as such. Even one of my good male friends recently said (quite definitively), "You don't like kids." Not having kids must equal not liking them. And there you have it.

The assumptions are vast. That I am so promiscuous I chose the 'free' life versus having kids is another. Although I don't 'read' this way, at this age I see a shift in men. They are bolder in their flirtations and innuendoes. As if to say, they know I did not choose the family life because I cannot contain my desires. That is their fantasy, not mine. It seems to go hand and hand with the childless card. Translated, this means it is so unnatural for a woman not to have children that I must not only be selfish but also one of those toxic aggressive types. For others, this neatly ties up the question of why I am single with no kids. Must be true…

So I did what many women in my shoes would do. I eventually started to play into it. Trying to act like I am a 'modern' free-sprit who chose this exciting and fulfilling life and would not have it any other way. As if this were a conscious, deliberate choice on my part. What else was I to say for myself? Admit how profoundly sad and empty I feel inside? This was never an option. And herein lies the problem. Women don't talk about this. So I assumed by their silence they echoed what I knew to be true – I missed the one road to contentment and true happiness.

Deep down I know being a mother would have agreed with me. Creating a life, nurturing it, loving it beyond all else. What could be better? For me it has been especially difficult not having children. For the obvious biological reasons and for the not so obvious societal ones. Everything is designed around women having kids. Activities are centered on kids. Mommy and me classes, being a PTA mom, a soccer mom - you get the picture. You have a built in social life when you have kids. Things to always do, friendships to continually make. For me the connections are few and far between. I have little in common with mothers. Well, let me rephrase that, they think I have nothing in common with them. So I don't get included in activities. This means the majority of women are out of my potential circle of friends. In turn, this means more isolation for me. I had no idea how this all worked.

It impacts everything. Your social life, how you are perceived, how you are treated, and, as a result, how you see yourself. As lesser than. Because that is how society is set-up. And women have some secret bond where they don't let you in on any other version of the story. They say motherhood is the best thing in their life. If you listen to any important figure of our time and they are asked to name their greatest accomplishment, what do they say - my children. Where does that leave me? Gee, my promotion at work? It is drilled into us time and time again this is the ONLY choice.

In my circle, no one ever lets you in on the fact you can be fulfilled without having kids. For many of us, it was circumstances, not a deliberate choice. Only recently has the mask dropped. Some friends have let it slip that having children is not all they expected it to be. It might not be the panacea or magic elixir I had thought it was. I don't delight in hearing this. But if I had known this earlier in life, if people were open to taking candidly about having or not having kids, what a difference this would have made. There is no one road, no absolutes.

"Things do not change, we do."
Henry David Thoreau

❧ Essay 2 ☙

Unlike many of my friends, I did not hold the assumption that I would become a mother. I was always puzzled and a bit envious of anyone who 'just knew' the path they wanted to take. For me, it was never a given. Even at an early age, I knew that motherhood was fraught with the highest of highs and the lowest of lows. I wasn't entirely against it, nor was I convinced it was right for me.

My mom is the most wonderful mother in the world. She was, and still is, my most loyal and best friend. But, she was dealt a difficult hand. She grew up in a time when any woman who wasn't married by age 20 was considered an old maid. The conventional wisdom was that a woman's life purpose was to be a mother. With a naïve impression of how she would live happily ever after, she married a charismatic alcoholic at age 19 and set up housekeeping. She always wanted to be a mother, and she often told my brother and me that given the choice, she would have had a whole house full of children. Being a good parent came naturally to her.

My experience of being an only child in the late 60's/early 70's was idyllic. It was my wonderful nuclear family – mom, dad, and me. We listened to Don McLean, Frank Sinatra, and The Beatles LPs on the record player and had a basset hound named Hombre. My dad went to graduate school while working for a startup retail chain. He and I watched Flip Wilson on TV. We would rake mounds of leaves in the back yard and go for bike rides. My mom was an accomplished artist and homemaker who canned (awful) pickles in the kitchen. I would regularly walk into the kitchen to find my parents engaged in a passionate embrace. Life was pretty close to perfect.

When I was four, life took a tragic turn. Tomas, my brother, was born on October 31, 1971 and died of sudden infant death syndrome on Christmas day the same year. This traumatic event turned our lives upside down. I remember that Christmas like it was yesterday. Both my parents still feel the anguish and pain from his loss.

In 1973, my mother gave birth to my brother, John. While in the hospital, both contracted a staph infection. Thankfully they recovered. John's survival depended upon his being bathed every few hours with special solution and being given tons of antibiotics to kill the infection. He's alive and well today.

Not long after John was born, my parents divorced – a common occurrence, it turns out, for parents of children who die from SIDS. Overnight, we went from living in a beautiful suburb surrounded by orange groves and having a stay-at-home mom and a dad who came home for dinner each night to living a completely different lifestyle. My mom, who only had a high school education, had to find a way to make a living to support us.

From then on, Mom, John, and I made our way. In the early years, my dad was around intermittently, but, in hindsight, he was more of a distraction and drain on my mom than he was helpful. In his alcoholic state, he constantly promised to pay child support, but little of it ever materialized. To us, he was affectionate, loving, and wonderful, but for my mom, it was a very different story. Over the years, I began to increasingly appreciate how challenging it was for her to make ends meet and keep us afloat. In the end, she always provided for us, often at the expense of her own mental and physical health. Why would that be an attractive path to follow? At no point had I officially decided not to be a mom, but it certainly seemed like something that you'd want to pursue with your eyes wide open. I also knew that single motherhood was a very real possibility.

As a teenager and young adult, the idea of motherhood was all around me, but it never fully attracted me. As more of my friends had children, I loved to hold and coo at them and then gleefully hand them back to their parents when they started to cry. It's not to say that I never considered being a mother, but it seemed like something that I might have to *endure*, as children continued to seem like a constant drain. I kept my concerns about motherhood mostly to myself because I realized they were politically incorrect. What kind of woman wouldn't want children? Isn't it natural to want a family? I felt inadequate and wrong for having doubts about motherhood. It's not that I didn't like kids or that I judged others negatively for having them, but I felt uncomfortable admitting to others that motherhood seemed unattractive to me.

Well-intentioned friends would often comment to me that I was going to be a good mother, and I knew it, too. If 'the universe' decided that I was to be a mother, I planned to embrace the situation and love my child, but, in my heart, I knew it was not going to be something I would actively pursue. I never wanted to admit the main reason I would even consider motherhood was because I worried about what a childless life would be like as an old woman. I've come to learn that having children neither guarantees happiness (every asshole has a mother), nor ensures you'll not be alone. The possibility of ending up alone can be anyone's fate, not just for those who are childless. All the same, through my 20's and early 30's, I was undecided and open to either possibility.

When I met my future husband, I soon learned he had already made the irreversible decision to not to have children; he had a vasectomy. When he proposed, I suddenly had to come to terms with how I felt about living a childless life. At that time, I lamented to my best girlfriend that if I chose to marry this man, I'd never know what it would be like to have children or to have the experience of giving birth to a child. I was worried that I was missing out on this essential life experience. She said that in becoming a mother, she'd never know what life would be like <u>without</u> having a child. She also said she would absolutely miss out on many of the things that my lifestyle, as a childless woman, would afford me. It was an epiphany. She opened my eyes to the fact that no one in life can have every possible experience and that motherhood is just one of many from which we can choose. "Don't make a decision out of a place of fear," she said to me. I realized that up until then, I didn't want to give myself permission to not have a child, when, in fact, I really didn't want to. I'm indebted to her for this insight, as it set my heart at ease.

Since then, several of my friends who are mothers have quietly admitted to me that, had they to do it over again, they might not have chosen to have children, or they confessed to envying the childless life. I tell them that sometimes I envy them, too; it's true.

From time to time, I've entertained the idea of adopting a child, but then I try to examine my reasons, and it all comes back to my fears of being alone. Is this really the right reason to be a mother? I don't think so.

So where am I today? I've been happily married to my husband for nine years. We've been blessed with a loving marriage and a full life of music, art, travel, and a constantly expanding circle of friends. So far, I'm confident I've made the right choices for me. I have special children in my life that give me an outlet to be an 'auntie'. I've got the best of both worlds.

"At some point your heart will tell itself what to do."
Achaan Chah

ɞ Essay 3 ʚ

Childless, or is it Childfree?

Some people are born with it, and some aren't. Some are brought up around it, and some aren't. Well I had neither the desire nor the instinct to be a mother.

At my Catholic high school, I was surrounded by friends, who had 4-8 siblings. They were aunts at the age of 12, and there were always babies around. My friends' mothers would "Ah" and "Goo" when a baby or toddler would come in the room.

This scene was so foreign to me. I was the youngest in my whole family, cousins included, so I didn't grow up with young ones around. My mother did not melt when babies were present. Actually, sometimes she displayed quite the opposite, such as by making some snide comment about how the person was too young to have a child.

A high school babysitting experience illustrates how foreign childrearing was to me. I recall my neighbors begging me to babysit their 5-7 year old boys. I said, "yes," reluctantly. When I had trouble getting the kids to listen to me, I called my mom for advice, but she couldn't help. I knew I could call my friend, Katy, who was a babysitting machine. Sure enough, she talked me through the night!

Later I married a wonderful, carefree man. When we married, we agreed to have children, and I kept thinking I would grow into the desire to have them. As my friends started to have children in their 20s and 30s, I was happy for them but still could not visualize myself being a full-time parent. However, I enjoyed being with my friends' and cousins' toddlers part-time.

To be even more frank, I can't say that I have ever enjoyed being around newborns to 1 year olds. Although it may sound strange, I think I am scared of them. Maybe I fear I would break them. Furthermore, I hate it when parents force you to hold their infants. Why would you do this to your child? I would not want to hand over my child to someone uninterested in holding him or her! Usually the room is full of others who want to hold babies. I am always in the minority!

My rule is this: When children can hold me back, I will hold them.

The older and more set in my ways I became, the further I got from the idea of being a mother. My husband was a man whose greatest desire was to have kids. He felt that childrearing was the only way to leave your legacy on earth. His giving the world many beautiful songs, works of art, homemade furniture, and unique ideas was not enough. Even though we were most compatible and loved each other dearly, the obstacle was still there – like an elephant in the room. IT just kept getting bigger and bigger. There was no way I would be able to make this person I loved happy without having a child, but I just could not make that turn. The bottom line is that my lack of maternal desire cost us our marriage.

He eventually found someone else with whom to spend his life, someone who shares his views about having children. He says, "It is just natural." I am happy he is going to be able to complete himself and is choosing to be happy. He will be a great father.

I, on the other hand, don't think I would have been a great mother. People say that is not true, but I think I know myself best. And maybe I played like a child. If I could not 'win' or be the best parent, then I did not want to play. Parenting is fraught with making mistakes and risking that this child you love so much will reject you. I think being a parent gives you a lifetime of love, and it also comes with as much hurt as it does love. It could be that I did not want to play in that sandbox.

Although I still can't visualize myself being a parent, it does not mean I don't like children. I love being around my nieces and nephews and friends' kids. I love talking and playing with them and hearing their ideas. I think this is an idea people can't grasp. "If you like kids, why don't you have some for yourself?" I can't give a good reason except the instinct is not there. Some would say it is self-centered, but at least I was able to identify my selfish tendencies and foresee the shortcomings of my having become a parent.

Everyone has children for different reasons, but I think a primary reason is to have family when you get older. Today, more people are choosing to not have children. I seem to have many of these child-free friends. I guess birds of a feather flock together. The joke is that we will all be living on a commune together without anyone to take care of us. Well, maybe that is where kids come in. I have a feeling we old birds will all be very childlike, and maybe we will be reflecting on our lives. Would we trade the house of old coots for a house full of kids? I guess time will tell, but for now, I have experienced loss because of my decision to be child-free, yet I feel no regret.

"Nobody has ever measured, even poets,
how much the heart can hold."
Zelda Fitzgerald

~ Essay 4 ~
MY TRIANGLE

Well, I can't honestly say I'm childless because I have four kids – three boys and one girl. I'm referring to my Labradors, but I can't imagine a stronger maternal love out there. And they would tell you they definitely have a mom.

I was never a 'baby' person. When growing up, friends of mine would see a baby and run to hold it and coo and would say they couldn't wait to have children themselves. Not me. That has never been my impulse, and it never entered my mind as one of my goals. I always wanted and needed dogs, though. Three, four, five…. I'd have ten if my husband would agree.

When I was single, I was so busy with career goals, friends and family, and volunteering that I never felt a time-clock ticking. My life was fulfilling and rich with strong and loving relationships. I felt no void. I was happy and satisfied being single and dating. I never felt that getting married would be an accomplishment, but I thought it sure would be nice if the right person and I found each other. Never did I feel that a child would be needed to make my life complete.

To have children, one needs to be willing to put them first in any situation and be willing to sacrifice any personal wants or needs for their benefit. Having children was committing to a lifelong financial responsibility that should not be considered lightly. To have children, potential parents should go through a grueling process of approval and should have to obtain a childbearing license. I, of course, would make myself available to approve or disapprove candidates. So many people make the decision to have (or keep) a child without anticipating the responsibility.

Most problems in the world would be solved if people took responsibility for themselves and their own actions. I have been standing on that soapbox for years, but I am responsible to a fault. It's been part of me for so long that I don't know when it started. It's built up and compounded. I am responsible for multiple jobs and the pressure of everything that goes with them: management, accounting, egos, scheduling, and bills; my parent's bills; constant reorganization of my house, my life, and my clients; chores; and deadlines for everything.

I feel responsible for relationships: my husband, my dogs, my friends, my family, my best friend's daughter, my troubled nephew, my friend who is engulfed in a horrible relationship, my best friend who has no other family, my aging friends who don't have many others left in their lives, anyone who would be alone on holidays, my neighbors, and in recent years, my aging parents.

I welcomed all these responsibilities. But I never yearned to be responsible for children. And I never felt that I wanted to devote the time necessary to raise children to my standards.

A friend describes my syndrome as "The Three P's" – Perfection, Procrastination, and Paralysis. This is the syndrome that overshadows my life in so many areas, but it basically is the concept that being so obsessed with perfection discourages any type of ultimate action.

I did not experience childbirth, and I am now forty-seven. It was a conscious choice, but when did it become a decision? I don't even know. Life happens and evolves, and here I am. With my husband and my dogs, I have a great family, and I am satisfied.

I never felt that I was interested enough to give that much of myself, my time, my energy, to commit to a child for the rest of my life. I had more than enough for which I was responsible. I have no problem taking on any other responsibility and overachieving at that, but the thought of having a child was and is overwhelming.

Sometimes I wonder what made me different from most others in that respect. Some women have great challenges conceiving, and having children becomes their main focus. And yet, I chose not to have kids when no physical challenge was in my way (as far as I know).

The concept I accept is that everyone has a personal triangle that makes him or her complete. Specific layers of aspects, or things salient to a person's life, fill the triangle, and they are arranged by priority in a hierarchy, where the most important aspects are at the top levels. The triangle is completely different for each individual. For some, religion might be at the top. A good portion of their triangle would be filled with religion, followed by other layers such as a secure relationship, humor, a satisfying career, and a multitude of other things they deem essential to their well-being.

Children are not in my triangle. Dogs, however, are a huge part of my triangle, right up there with my husband. I think my dogs fulfill any maternal instincts I may have. Everyday I get the most joy interacting with them, caring for them, and communicating with them.

When my friend read my chakras, she had a vision of a past time. A woman in old-fashioned dress with a lacy, high-collared blouse and long dark hair was overseeing a picnic at a carnival, caring for everyone present. Kids of all ages were running around, and a dog was romping with them. For a second, I thought about the woman and the lace; then I asked if I could be the dog in her vision.

As it turned out, the dog had originally been the strongest image in her vision, but she kept trying to put it out of her mind and focus on the woman.

Is it weird that dogs elicit powerful emotions in me, whereas I feel neutral toward a child?

I am confident that I could have and would have been a good mother because I would have fulfilled the responsibility. But without passion for childrearing, it would have not been fair to the child. I am 100% positive I am giving my dogs the best life experience possible, and I love every second of it!

What a great triangle I have, even if there is a "P" at each corner!

"I think that these difficult times have helped me to understand better than before how infinitely rich and beautiful life is in every way and that so many things that one goes around worrying about are of no importance whatsoever."
Isak Dinesen

ೞ Essay 5 ೕ

Through all my years on this planet, I have consciously (and unconsciously) made the decision to not have children. To take it one step further… generally, I don't even have children around me as a potential substitute for what they give: their free will, energy, truthfulness, humor, or any of the joys associated with a child. Please do not misunderstand; I do love children very much. I just don't have them around in my day-to-day life. Many wonder and/ or even criticize how I can be like this. My response is: "This is who I am, and this is where I live at the moment."

Through the years I have wondered why I have no children in my life… childless. To me, the word "childless" implies that one is lacking or without, as if it would make a person whole to have a child or less than whole to be without a child. I personally believe there are many ways to become complete with or without children.

At this point in my life, I have covered every part of this debatable topic. I was married and did not have a child. I was in a serious relationship where it was a very real possibility to have a child. We even discussed it, but, again, I chose against it. Was I just too busy in my own life to share at the time? Was my partner? Was it completely selfish to choose to not want to share? Was it because I was self-deprecating many hours of the day and couldn't fathom putting that on a child? Was I just being rebellious because society and peers were telling me I needed a child to be a 'normal' person? Are there just too many children in the world starving and homeless? The questions go on and on.

I am in what I feel is an uncommon situation, where I have no children and neither do any of my siblings. My parents would love to have grandchildren, but to their sadness, there are none. I feel some guilt over this and sometimes wish that one of my siblings would have a child to carry on our family. It doesn't appear to be in the cards.

I have no doubt I will never bear a child. I am neither sad, nor do I feel any loss over this concept. In fact, my medical insurance does not even cover having a baby! The only recent switch in my current mentality and comfort zone is the possible desire to adopt a child. I ask myself if this inclination is for selfish reasons, or is it because I truly want to nurture and raise a child. Very likely, it is a little of both, and I know there are too many kids in the world that need love and good homes. We will see what happens.

Some people choose to have many children.

Some people are desperately sad because they physically cannot.

Some people desire children and their partners do not.

Some people are willing to alter the laws of nature to have children.

And...

Some people are completely content and happy without ever going through the labors of bearing a child.

"Remember always that you have not only the right to be an individual you have the obligation to be one."
Eleanor Roosevelt

➧ Essay 6 ➨

When I was asked to write why I made the choice to not have children, I have to admit I didn't know what to say. As I sit here, I am still unsure of my reasons. I can say for certain that I have never wanted children. Even as a child, I was positive I never wanted to be a mother.

However, when I was 15 years old, my mom had my younger brother. It seemed overnight I went from would-be sister to surrogate mother, from caring for a sick crying baby to the joy of watching him take his first steps. I moved on to spending parent hours in the elementary school classroom, chaperoning fieldtrips, volunteering at school carnivals, going to sports practice, assisting with homework, attending sports games, and the list goes on. My brother/son is in college, and I can say with complete certainty that I do not want any children.

I'm a 33 year-old African-American. I work, spend lots of time in the gym, and have friends and family. I want to embrace as much of life as I possibly can. Is it selfish? Yes. I want a life without the responsibility of bringing a life into this world, to be able to live my life on my own terms, to travel and make love often.

Still, when asked, people tell me without fail, "You just haven't met the right man yet. When you fall in love, you'll want to have children." I have heard that statement all my life. When do I get to mean what I say? At what age do I get to be taken seriously?

And what if my critics are wrong?

I remember hearing Dr. Laura's radio show once when a lady called in to say she and her husband were having problems because she didn't want to have children and her husband had changed his mind and now wanted them. Dr. Laura's response was that this woman was selfish, that she would not become a real woman until she gave birth because that is why we are here on the planet. She was so insanely rude and mean to this poor woman. All I could think was, "Why does it have to mean anything other than not wanting to have children?"

Listening to that crazed rant brought up some of my insecurities about that very thing. Do I deserve to be loved? Is it wrong for me to ask someone to love me when I don't want to have kids? Will I end up keeping someone from having what he wants? I have always been up front in telling my romantic partners that I do not want to have children. I never want to mislead anyone. Nonetheless, I can't shake the feeling that somehow I am wrong.

You can be loving, giving, and nurturing without having kids.

Could the reason be that I think the world is crazy now, and to bring children into such uncertainty is unfair? Or that there are more than enough children waiting to be adopted and loved, so I don't need to have my own when I can give my love to one in need?

I can also say that it is not because I dislike kids; in fact, I love them. The sound of their laughter is one of the happiest sounds in the world.

"I have forged my own life, but not alone; my friends
have made the better part of it."
Shawna Corley

‽ Essay 7 ‿

CHILD-LESS OR CHILD-FREE?

According to *Webster's Encyclopedia Unabridged Dictionary of the English Language*, a "child" is:
1. A boy or girl.
2. A son or daughter.
3. Any person or thing regarded as the product or result of particular agencies, influences, etc.

From the same dictionary, "less" means:
1. An adjective suffix meaning "without" and, in adjectives derived from verbs, indicating failure or inability to perform or be performed.
2. Free from, without, false.

And last but not least, "free" means:
1. Pertaining to or reserved for those who enjoy personal liberty.
2. Unimpeded, unattached.

What does it actually mean to be "child-less" or "child-free"? Am I less of a person because I'm without a son or daughter? Or am I actually an unimpeded person who enjoys personal liberty?

I did not intend to be childless. I always thought I would have children because that's what people do when they grow up and get married. I had even picked out names for the children I would have.

Unfortunately, I was unable to have my own children due to

various circumstances. Even though I did not get married until I was close to 40, my husband and I decided to start a family. We went through several medically assisted attempts to have our own children but were ultimately unsuccessful. According to a very condescending doctor, it was for no good reason other than we were "too old." Of course I was angry, and I raged that it was completely unfair.

How come I was always told that if you wanted something badly enough and worked hard for it, then it was always attainable? Why wasn't pregnancy happening for me? Maybe I really didn't want children. Maybe I was not 'visualizing' myself being a mother. Maybe I didn't have the right doctor, acupuncturist, herbs, diet, drugs, and/or exercise regimen. And what about my husband? How come he wasn't cutting down on caffeine and exercising more? Did he really want children? Why were we told as young people how easy it is to get pregnant? How come I was now spending money to have a kid when it was supposed to be 'free'? What would happen if I got a dud of a kid after spending all that money?

Well, after much soul-searching and crying about my situation, I realized that maybe it really was a blessing in disguise to not have children. Because of our journey through infertility, we were able to refocus on why we married each other in the first place. We talked about other options but decided that adoption and egg donation were not for us. Once we overcame this hurdle, it was like being relieved of a great weight. No longer did we have to think about/worry about our children being bullied, or not getting picked for a team, or getting into drugs. We did not have to worry about how to pay for college or how we might somehow psychologically damage them.

So, getting back to being childless or child-free…. We are definitely without a son or daughter, *and* we are also unimpeded by not having to care for our own children.

But as far as being childless, I'm not sure that I would actually call myself that. I have many children in my life, so my life is not without children. I just don't have my own. And though it would have been nice to see what kind of person my husband and I could have created together, we are just as happy to have each other's company. In the end, it's your partner with whom you create a life, not your children. You give life to children, but they grow up and create their own lives. Whatever decision people make about kids, it's not something that should be taken lightly or without consideration.

"Each of us has a choice about how to love
the world in our own unique way."
Bernie Siegel MD

Essay 8

I married at the end of December 1998. I left my family and my job to be with my husband who was transferred to another state. Within one month my period was late, and I thought I was pregnant. I was so lonely and needy that I was actually thrilled at the prospect – not realizing what a huge responsibility this thing would be. I was not pregnant after all. When I think back, I thank God for that one.

The following month I confided in my mother-in-law about the event. We discussed the fact that my father-in-law was sterile but managed to get my mother-in-law pregnant. I knew this information already, but she felt the need to repeat it, as if my husband and I were not doing everything right. She said she really wanted a grandchild. Thereafter, she began tracking my periods, which I thought was weird. She called certain times of the month to tell me when I was fertile and reminded me to have sex and to do so quickly since my husband's job required extensive travel. I never became pregnant. She was disappointed, which I understood, but she treated me differently and made comments about giving up on being a grandmother. As a result, our relationship suffered, and I grew to dislike her.

In the meantime, my sister gave birth. It was a life-changing event for my entire family. We were all thrilled. As I mentioned earlier, I moved to a different state with my husband, so I would visit my family at Christmas.

My first visit after the birth of her son was an eye-opener. My sister, as well as the rest of my family, assumed that I knew how to care for an infant. They looked at me like I was a freak when I was uncertain about how to hold the baby, change him, etc.

They would say things like, "What? Are you kidding me? How could you not know? It's instinctual. A woman just knows these things." "Not this woman," I thought.

Eventually my family realized I needed instruction and laughed a little. I felt like an outsider in my mother's home. Questions and comments followed. "Why aren't you having children? Are you having problems? You would be such a good mother. Hey, maybe you should adopt or see a fertility specialist." I never had the right answers.

No one listened anyway. I know that because I was asked the same questions for three years straight. The saddest part is that I am not as important in my family because I am not a mother. My life and experiences about which my family once asked have been overshadowed by the experiences of the mothers and mothers-to-be in my immediate family.

At the same time, my mom gets it. I am not a mother, and that is fine with her. It wasn't meant to be. End of story.

I will refrain from going on and on about the mothers in the outside world and how they treat us, the childless ones, differently. It would take too long. However, I will say that I am not a member of their club, and I feel it.

Lastly, that I am not a mother makes me no less of a woman.

I embody all of the beautiful qualities of a mother.

I just don't have children.

Love to all of you.

"Being deeply loved by someone gives you strength, while loving someone deeply gives you courage."
Lao Tzu

∞ Essay 9 ☙

What is it like to be childless? How did this happen to me? I wanted six children. To be more specific, I wanted five boys and one girl in that order. I wanted to be married by age twenty-five, teach kindergarten for three years, and then start cranking out babies.

Reality: I had one train wreck of a relationship after another from the time I turned twenty-four to the time I turned thirty-eight. I, for the most part, dated men who were commitment phobic. When I finally married at age thirty-eight, I felt relieved that I was finally going to get to be a mother. WRONG! My husband left me alone to travel on 'business' six out of seven days a week, and he was NOT a bit interested in 'amorous relations'. How in the heck did this happen? While we were dating and then later engaged, he expressed that he wanted children, too. He wanted a big family just like I did. He wanted me to be a stay at home mother. We had a three-story house by the beach. He had a great job and made good money; we did not want for any material items. I did not sign up for this! What was happening? I cried every day, multiple times a day for two and a half years and finally divorced the creep after a year's plus of couple's counseling.

I married for the second time at age forty-three and am EXTREMELY happy. But how can that be? I don't have any children. My dream never came true, or did it?

A few months before I married my current husband, I was sweeping off my screened-in front porch. Sunbeams were shining down on it at an angle I had never seen before. An overwhelming sense of peace and calm washed over me, and I felt euphoric. It only lasted for a few seconds, but I remember feeling immediately afterwards that if I could bottle the feeling I just felt, I could be a millionaire. I sat down and tried to recapture the experience, but I couldn't revive it. I teared up, but I couldn't cry. I felt so joyful I just wanted to cry or leap or fly, but all I could do was stand there, holding my broom. While I didn't hear a large booming voice come from the sky or anything like that, the message that I received while those feelings washed over me was this, "You prayed to be a mother. You thought I didn't hear you, but I did. You are not the kind of mother that you prayed to be. You are the kind of mother that I want you to be. You are the kind of mother who helps other people with their children." I remember feeling so relieved and peaceful that I never looked back and have never regretted not being a mother in the traditional sense of the word.

I was a teacher for thirteen years, a Marriage Family Therapist Intern for five years, and am currently an elementary school counselor. I have truly been helping other mothers with their children since I was thirteen years old! I believe the reason for my success is that I DO NOT have children of my own. Not having children of my own affords me the energy to listen with love, patience, and understanding to the students and parents who come to see me. I approach each day with renewed vigor and positive anticipation. I do not have distractions at home that get in my way of 'mothering'.

I will never be called "mommy," "mom," "mama," "mother," "grandma," or "great grandma." I don't have any biological children to take care of me when I'm old, and that scares me a little bit and makes me a little sad. BUT…I have a loyal and long list of former students who love me and will always be there for me in my old age. It's not the children we give birth to from our own bodies, but the children we nurture along the way that makes us mothers.

"It is possible to be different and still be alright."
Anne Wilson Schaef

ॐ Essay 10 ☙

I am a thirty-seven year old woman, and I am not a mother. As a young girl, motherhood felt like an identity reserved for those who knew something I didn't. They learned the secrets afforded by secure love and a happy family life. My sense of family shattered when I turned three. All five of my half-siblings vanished. According to my parents, they were "wicked disappointments, rebellious vermin." In addition, my mother reminded me daily of how my birth destroyed her body, particularly her once-beautiful legs, now riddled with snake-like veins. I feared her fate, so I started policing my body, too – at the ripe age of three. Emblazoned in my being was the message: *Children destroy your life*.

That Christmas, I received a baby doll and Barbie. To this day, I recall feeling afraid as I looked at the baby doll. She appeared weak and vulnerable in her pink lace outfit. I hated her, which precipitated sadness and guilt. She was innocent, was she not? Disturbed by my confusion, I decided she would stay in her box, neglected. I could not love her. I would not love her because I could not love myself. It wasn't safe. Instead, I picked up Barbie, who promised me beauty, strength, and acceptance. Moreover, I was certain she had no children. In Ken, she hoped to find love, while I went undetected.

In this atmosphere of shame and fear, I not only repressed my maternal instinct, but my body belied a more tragic tale. The age of puberty arrived without my blossoming into womanhood. Becoming a fully developed, sexual woman was even more dangerous than being a child. When I fell in love at age twenty-two, my first menstrual cycle appeared. I married at age twenty-three, only to discover I had married a monster. He cursed my body and my womanhood. He was my mirror into what I had become to myself. Any latent desires I had to become a mother remained hidden. My menses ceased for seven years, as survival took precedence over bearing children. Then I broke free, not only from the institution of marriage, but also from the loveless legacy of my family of origin.

> *There came a time when the risk to remain tight in the bud was more painful than the risk it took to blossom.*
> *~ Anais Nin*

With relentless determination, *I* developed. My body became fertile as my sense of self took root, as I became the lover of my own body and soul. I questioned and re-narrated every story that held me hostage as a female, let alone as an adult woman. With humility and gratitude, my purpose emerged – to become a life midwife to those who are ready and willing to birth their own unfettered identities into this manifest realm. Trained as a Marriage and Family Therapist and Certified as an Integral Coach, I have been living in alignment with my native wisdom ever since, and I am deeply honored to help others do the same.

Nonetheless, as I sit with who I have become, maternal longings arise. They feel both foreign and familiar. Am I too late? For a moment, I feel myself holding my own baby in my arms, and I weep. As this sadness recedes, my awareness turns to the responsibilities of motherhood. Suddenly, I feel dread, as if I were a bird about to have her wings clipped – forever. It's taken her so long to take flight. How could she possibly allow herself to go back into a cage? Quieting my mind and soothing my heart, I reconcile that I am, indeed, doing enough. I am a childless woman, and *I am* already enough.

"Spread your love everywhere you go."
Mother Teresa

ಐ Essay 11 ಔ

I have never had children but interact with many on a daily basis. I write this essay while waiting to help my friend's eight-year old with his extra credit art project and her ten-year old daughter with her fifth grade history assignment. I became a tutor for kindergarteners while in the fifth grade and have been tutoring children ever since. I also caretake for my friends' children when asked. My life is full of children – watching my friends' kids, volunteering on behalf of organizations for children, and being a Big Sister, a role I've held for twenty-five years. Childless I am not.

I grew up spending summers with my grandparents who I adored and who adored me. They taught me how to ice-skate and how to ride my bike. They took me to museums and played board games such as cribbage and monopoly with me. Recently, a father of two girls, six and eight years old, told me he had the best time being a single uncle and that being a father was different in a more restrictive way. I think that I skipped the role of mother and have taken over the role of a non-related 'grandmother' - one who takes friends' children ice-skating, bakes them cookies, and plays board games with them.

I cherish this role.

My sister and her husband chose never to have children because they often travel worldwide. They chose not to pursue the option available to them – to have a child who lives with a nanny once a month or more. They love their careers and the international life they chose.

Like me, they are godparents but not parents. They are happy, too.

Had I met my soulmate, married him, and had a child, I would have enjoyed the experience immensely. However, the man of my dreams has not yet appeared, and having children of my own is unlikely.

I am at peace knowing that my life is as it is supposed to be.

"Write it on your heart that every day
is the best day of the year."
Ralph Waldo Emerson

ᛞ Essay 12 ⌘

DOES BEING 'CHILDLESS' MEAN BEING 'WITHOUT'?

Ever since I can remember, I have always known I never wanted kids unless I was married. I love kids. I knew one day I would get married and raise a family of my very own. I would marry someone fabulous, and we would live happily ever after in our white picket-fenced home. My husband and I would have two children, a dog, a cat, and a rose garden. Well, my fairytale life hasn't materialized… yet…or maybe it won't….

My choices in selecting a potential husband and father haven't been the best. At some point during my various relationships, I realized the man I was dating wasn't the right fit. We would never make it as a couple. The relationship wasn't right for me. I TRIED REALLY hard to make a few of my relationships work, but it was like putting a square peg into a round hole. Not good; not good at all. Don't ask me how I knew these men weren't right. I just knew.

I feel like I have been on this constant search to find the 'right' man who will marry me and want to have a family with me. I was told a man is supposed to take care of me – financially, sexually, and emotionally. I was also told I had to know how to take care of myself. Reconciling these conflicting messages has proven challenging and has affected how I show up in relationships. My track record has proven to me that I keep selecting men who didn't want to be married or have children…at least not with me.

I have been preventing myself from having what I wanted - a husband and family. I have been my own condom - my very own preventative measure. I have been so fearful of making the wrong decision, of falling in love with the wrong man who could be my 'happily ever after'. I never wanted to be divorced — EVER. Being a child from a divorced family, I never wanted to re-experience that much pain. I also have been so fearful of failing as a parent. What if I don't teach the child the proper manners and social skills? What if I am not nurturing enough? I don't want my child to do drugs or become a criminal. My giving in to so much fear is why I am my very own condom! I am not sure why I am so fearful of failing. I know life has no guarantees — whether regarding marriage, parenting, or anything else for that matter.

So here I am 45 years later, 'childless'. But, I really don't view myself as being childless. The word 'less' means 'lack of'. I don't feel any lack in my life. I feel 'rich' in so many other areas of my life. How do you know if you are really truly missing something if you don't know what you don't have? Having a child is a huge responsibility. I guess I haven't wanted to be a parent that badly to embark on the journey of parenting. Obviously, parenting wasn't meant to be part of my life path. Other lessons, people, and experiences have taken center stage. I am grateful for how my life has unfolded thus far.

I now believe that my being childless has been both a conscious and subconscious decision. Consciously, had I REALLY wanted to be a mother, I could and would have been. I am blessed with a great support network, which includes family and friends who would love and support my decision. Subconsciously, I have selected men with whom I knew I could not create a long-term relationship or family. I am proud that I honored my own beliefs and values, that I didn't settled down with just any man so I could have a husband and family. I am also proud of not conforming to society's dictate that women are 'supposed' to bare children. I am not making excuses; I just don't care what others think, nor do I give in to their pressure.

I have been blessed that my parents have never pressured me to get married, let alone have a child. My mother's philosophy is, "Do what is right for you, and be with the person who is appropriate for you." I could still be a single mom IF I really wanted to. I just don't want to. So I have made the choice and settled with the decision that I probably won't be a mother. But heck… I am a GREAT aunt! I am "Auntie" to many kids in my life. So really… I'm not childless.

"We all have the power to give away love, to love other people. And if we do so we change the kind of person we are, and we change the kind of world we live in."
Rabbi Harold Kushner

❧ Essay 13 ☙

At seventeen I was working in a free medical clinic. I talked with the doctors about tubal ligation. They all said they wouldn't take me as a patient. They all said I would change my mind.

And then it was there. The clear, steady pang – the call to motherhood. It surprised me.

At twenty-three it all seemed a necessary part of the picture. With no man in sight in the midst of this persistent pang, I became a nanny. I lived in my friend's guest house; she was a single mom raising an eight-year old daughter. My friend was a devoted mother, growing organic gardens and carpooling and feeding her toddler one raisin at a time. But she began chomping at the bit to join the working world. So, we traded places. Logistically, it was easy. Emotionally, it was a train wreck. Although her daughter was a great kid, I soon became overwhelmed by the steady rhythm of her demand and need! She was easy and sweet and smart and funny. I was flattered when people referred to her as my daughter. I could imagine a slight resemblance. But the day in, day out nature of caretaking overtook my capacity for giving. Something about the birth and growth process prepares you for baths and meals and homework and bedtime stories that surrogacy does not. I hadn't done the coursework and was failing badly. After a few months, I relented. I couldn't handle what felt like a huge responsibility. I wondered about providing for the well being of another person. I had no idea how to handle it.

My friend called her mother to the rescue so she could continue climbing the ladder of financial success, while I was relieved of my duties. Whew!

At thirty-five, I married a man who decided to have a vasectomy while we were dating. He knew he didn't want kids, and I thought this was the responsible thing to do based on his feelings. I was naïve enough to believe that his decision didn't necessarily preclude my having children. I hadn't altogether decided against having children.

For years I worked in horticulture. Once while on the job with a landscaping crew, I got a ride back to the office with one of my co-workers, a young Hispanic man. We were chatting on the way back when he asked how many kids I had. I said, "none." He got very quiet and said sincerely, "I'm sorry." My heart sank. I knew he meant it, and I knew by the way he spoke that his children had greatly enriched his life. I felt sorrowful regret. In his culture, no matter your job or marital status, you have *kids-familia*. Again, I felt the pang of longing.

My hope of attaining motherhood expired long ago. However, two wonderful children have adopted me as their surrogate auntie. Through and with them I am discovering the immense grace that children bestow. They are beautiful and loving and generous with their wisdom.

I realize having a child would have altered my disposition to worry. I don't mean that I would have been spared grief or worry; rather, somehow a worldview expands when it includes another. From where I stand now, it all seems worth it.

Next week is Halloween. I get to see my dumplings. We will carve pumpkins. Life is sweet.

"We don't make mistakes. We just have learnings."
Anne Wilson Schaef

Essay 14

A Childless Mother

Looking over my life, I can remember always wanting to have three sons and a POWERFUL Black husband, whom I could respect and honor, and with whom I could grow old. I never wanted a daughter just because I was a rough-edged woman, and I did not want to raise my daughter like me. I wanted a son so that I could teach him all the things about which I read and believed. I wanted to show him what a young man should strive for in his life: devoting himself to raising a family, fearing GOD, and building up a good name.

To see my son love his father and want to be like him is something about which I fantasized. I wanted my young man to change households, communities, and then the nation. Then I could grow old with a smile on my face. But I woke up and realized my life wasn't the Cosby show…L.O.L.

At the age of nine or ten, I had my first sexual experience, and by the age of eleven or twelve, I learned that unwanted sex would turn all of my dreams into nightmares, my hopes to shame, and my trust to fear. It took away the emotion that would have enabled me to be a virtuous woman – all for a moment of pleasure. I was left with a lifetime of wounds that awaited healing. Men hated me until they wanted sex, at which point they suddenly talked nicely to me. When a person is violated sexually, intercourse takes on a different meaning. Sex becomes distorted with every touch and every proposition.

I felt I had no one to tell, so I kept it inside for many years, growing and developing into a woman with unshed tears. As a young person, I cried out in silence, but no one paid attention to the changes that took place in me. My silent cry always sounded when a man solicited me. I would never bring a child into this world where school, church, and family take advantage of children and steal their dreams by touching, grabbing, and caressing before the innocent understand what those movements mean. They're left with facing pain and pleasure!!!

How can a child process emotions meant for adults to share? I moved through life with the cares of the world on my shoulders.... I wanted to protect every child I knew from the pain I had to endure throughout my life....

As a teen, I liked boys who didn't like me because I looked like the monster living inside me. I felt like the world could see what I felt, so I wore my hurt like a defense shield, fending off everyone. I prayed for the day when I could be like each one of my friends. I wanted to have my innocence back. All of my friends were dating and going crazy over boys. I laughed and acted crazy over them, as well, all the while hoping they would never ask me out because of the words I heard behind closed doors: fat ass, stinky, dirty, ugly, stupid, and the phrase that held on like glue on a nail, "No man will ever want you except the ones from prison because only men from prison date fat girls." I heard that phrase and froze up every time I was alone with a man or when one showed he was attracted to me. These things still haunt me.

I asked myself if having a baby would change my life. Everyone I know who had children felt a love that was fresh and new, but the daddy problems were too much for me to bare, so having a baby with a dead beat father was not for me. I had a real vision of how my first babe's world would be.... All of my friends were telling their boyfriends stories, and I just cried inside, "Lord, I just want to be normal!" Walking around with my hair undone, my clothes a mess, and my weight out of control. What to do? Who to turn to? I felt ashamed all the time. I hated being unnoticed, and I was too afraid to open my mouth because most of the time others pushed me away and talked about me.

My family members were God-fearing people who went to church. I remember hearing a sermon preached on a Sunday morning at one of Pasadena's local churches. The preacher got up and began to teach. He said something that changed my whole life in a moment. I remember his words like it was yesterday. He roared like a lion and moved across the pulpit with so much authority, everyone hanging on his every word. Then he declared this life-altering statement, "Rape isn't rape unless you scream!" At that point, my mind, emotions, and body froze. I went home and vowed never to speak about my monsters again, even though they came after me by wiggling my toes, signaling a sneak attack on my mind, body, and soul, which are connected to my memory, emotions, and my vision for my life. It has taken me years to unfold, to come out of this hole, and to feel desire for having a child to hold.

I attempted to have a child with a friend with whom I had a lot in common. We wanted to bring a life into the world together. We didn't want to be a family, nor did we think about the impact our decision might have on our child. We just knew we were cool with one another, and that's all we needed from each other.

Long story short, I didn't get pregnant, and that was okay. Maybe it was God's will because our lives went down two different roads, and neither one of us looked back to check on one another. I would have been left alone to raise a child like 50 million other women in this world. God knows that is not what I wanted for myself, to be a single parent. But, if that was the deal, I would have created a loving life, full of caring, sharing, gentleness, and kindness, all of which would have made for a successful and prosperous life for my child. After this page turned on my life, I never wandered down that road again....

My life became full with godchildren, youth, family, and the children of friends.... My house was a place where young people came to be free and to be themselves. They learned about courage, fear, fun, laughter, and, simply put, how to be a child.

Parents sometimes forget how it is to be a child, and, therefore, godparents, youth leaders, and coaches become the exciting component in a child's life. Parents are no longer the ones to whom a child looks for joy. Parents – this pattern has got to change. Balance life with fun. Continue to pay the bills, go to the store, cook dinner, discipline, but whatever you do, don't forget when you were a child!!!!! Have fun, make them laugh, hang out together, give lots of hugs and kisses.... This advice goes for fathers, as well. And remember, fathers don't babysit, nor do they watch their children.... They take care, spend time, and make memories.

A woman without a child.... You must hear her story first before you judge her childless heart, clutching her will to bring life.

The word "mother" means, "a biological and/or social female parent of an offspring." A woman without a child longs for the touch of a child's small hand, a toothless smile, and the smell of Johnson and Johnson filling the room. They question their commitment to a young life and their womanhood. Children are a gift from God, so we, as childless women, understand how to handle this great gift sent from above. I wish for motherhood like every other woman without a child. I pray for the mother who has been honored to have a child, that they will live up to the responsibility placed in their hands.

A childless woman has a lot of regrets, shame, and sadness in her heart.... To love her is to take on all of her. Her silence, her laughter with a tear or two hanging on the edge of her eyelid, her lonely moments, the times when she's carefree and footloose.... To love her is to take on all of her.

God has seen me through all of my downswings and upswings. I have become a mother to many and a godmother, as well. I have a host of godchildren, sons, and daughters, and I show love to them all year-round. I give them everything I would give to my very own children. I became a childless mother against my choice but by God's will. I had a chance to be a mom, but I never birthed a child from my womb. God gave me a gift, and I have cherished it all the days of my life. What gift did he give, you ask? He gave me the gift of a mother's heart, and just like I can't explain my gifting fully, no one will ever be able to completely explain the spirit of a MOTHER, nor why a child clings to the heart of a MOTHER, whether she's loving or not....

The Words of a childless MOTHER... **God Bless the child who has a loving MOTHER.**

Dear God, give mothers a vision to guide their children with love and kindness, and, most importantly, give them the wisdom to instruct them in the right direction. Amen.

"The love we desire is already within us."
A Course in Miracles

ॐ Essay 15 ॐ

CHILDLESS IN A WORLD OF KIDS

I'm 58, single, and childless. I have been pregnant and have not been married. Call it fate, call it fortunate or unfortunate; this is what has happened. I never chose this scenario, one way or another. What I did choose was the dream of a family: a husband, a couple of kids (at least one son seemed natural), some pets, neighborhood barbeques, cocktail parties with smart martinis, lots of socializing with couples, travel, play-dates for the kids, etc. You might say I visualized the perfect Barbie and Ken existence that had nothing to do with the way I was raised or the life I have since led.

I did choose to end each pregnancy. In one case the relationship ended, and in the other, I couldn't picture a permanent tie with that particular lover. He was fun and smart but notoriously ungenerous, uncommunicative, and…well, kind of whiny. In other words, he was fun date material, not marriage material. Plus, I was pretty young and pretty much at sea emotionally.

The other alternative: raising a child alone with no support seemed completely out of the question. I know women who have had to raise kids on their own because of divorce, and they have had huge struggles. The women I've known who have chosen to have a child or children alone have at least had either family or some kind of financial support. Still, they are often pushed to their limits with having no partner for backup (or even to blame). I can't imagine that life. I don't look at their kids and feel sadness or regret about my own life.

Ironically, my birth mother had me out of wedlock and adopted me out. In those days, I don't imagine it was an easy option to choose abortions. Does that change my thinking about abortion in general? No. You might ask, "But what if you'd never been born?" My philosophy is, "When a soul wants to be born, it finds a way." I would have found a way.

I look around at my friends who have children and grandchildren, and I am of the mind that it would be nice to have that potential hedge against loneliness and aging without support, but those are not reasons to have children. What I do miss is a life partner, which I don't have right now. But that's another issue entirely.

I knew a woman who had a solid marriage and two grown children. But even decades after the fact, she still longed for the child she aborted before she was married. She told me her story while clearly filled with unresolved sadness and a palpable loneliness I could only understand viscerally, not intellectually. She was very bright, was one of the wealthiest women in California at the time I knew her, had a substantial extended family, and had access to any kind of therapy she needed. She died suddenly of a heart attack, but I think it had an emotional basis that had to do with that unhealed wound. Children may fill a womb for a few months, but they do not fill an empty soul. If I've learned anything at all, I've become aware of the wonders and mystery of life and the gift of being on a path of self-awareness. Giving birth and raising children may be one way to understand and experience love and deeper emotions, but it's only one of many opportunities we can create.

"Do not wait for life. Do not long for it. Be aware, always and at every moment, that the miracle is in the here and now."
Marcel Proust

✥ Essay 16 ✥

I always knew I would have children.

I was sure of it.
Absolutely and completely.
100% faith in the fact I would be a mom with a completely stereotypical 60's sitcom TV family: dad, kids, dog, home…the package.

I loved babysitting, and I was booked solid through high school and college. Seriously, I was booked every weekend for months ahead of time. I went on vacation with families and watched their kids. I moved into families' homes when the parents went traveling abroad. I adore kids. I love their energy. I love their honesty. I love to laugh and play. I love helping kids know they are unique and unlimited.

In high school, I also began my volunteer career working with children at a hospital. I also spent 12 years of my career working as a child advocate at a kids' nonprofit.

So, you get the idea. I love kids.

And I knew I would meet a man who wanted to create kids with me.

I was sure of it.
Absolutely and completely.
I never, ever, ever wanted to have a child without a man. Ever. It's a team job for me. And let's face it; I am really good with the

sugar, face-painting, and loving. I'm not so great with setting boundaries and helping with algebra, biology, or history.... So, I knew the best way I could launch healthy kids was to partner with a man and parent together under one roof.

I have friends who have the courage and confidence to be single parents.

I have friends who chose to have children with men who are fathers but not life partners.

No judgment.

There's certainly no right way to do it, but I was always really clear that we, this guy and I, would create our kids and have a family in the context of our undying love.

And then I fell in love.

Really and truly in love. Like we all do. And there's nothing like it. To feel safe, sexy, and secure was the best, best, best. To be myself and honored for that. He was awesome, and we laughed a lot.

And it was really grand...for awhile.

But to cut to the chase, when we were making love, it became incredibly clear to me that our connection was supposed to create a life. Our connection was supposed to make babies. I just felt it.

My guy told me our sex took him to a very spiritual place. After we made love, he would say he felt totally "complete." All good and happy.

Love, friendship, a home, some dogs, a nice garden....

We had it all.... But....

After about two years of making love without making babies, I found myself crying alone in my car as I drove down the freeway. It was the kind of crying where you really shouldn't be driving, the kind of crying where something very deep down inside is aching to be heard.

After one of my crying drives from San Diego to Los Angeles, I decided to end Us. When he said, "You told me I was more important than the dream of having a kid," all I could do was tell him, "I changed my mind."

Yeah, I know. In that moment, I sucked. The situation sucked. He sucked for not changing his mind about having a baby with me.

And, guess what, ten years later, I ended up childless. And it was very, very painful because the life I envisioned never came to pass. And that's when I had to be really honest with myself.

And that's when I decided to let go.

And this letting go is what helped me get past the pain. And when I say let go, I mean I let go.

I let go of all my false hopes and expectations. I let go of living in the future. I let go of the anger I felt toward myself for not having a baby. I let go of what everyone else was saying about my life.

And…

I started living in the present, living in the here and now.

And this living in the present is what helped me find my happiness again.

Through this process, life has sent me wonderful lessons in the form of people whom I have met along the way. I had the opportunity to meet people who have gone through incredibly hard times and ended up on the other side, filled with joy.

People like Maurice, who told me he made a pact with God if he survived World War II. His battalion was surrounded and under siege, gunfire everywhere. He said that if he could survive and go home to his wife in San Diego, he would never complain again. And guess what, after the war, he kept his pact until he passed away at the age of 92.

People like three female friends whose children died. I see these moms laugh. I see them get up everyday and go out and help others in their community. I see them still loving themselves and others.

People like my friend in a wheelchair. As a senior in high school, he was in a car crash that left him paraplegic. He is now married and is one of the happiest, coolest people with whom you could ever hang out. He has a wheelchair for the beach. He goes camping. Nothing ever stops him.

I didn't find the right man with whom to have a child.

It happens.

Shit happens. Seriously, sometimes this is the absolutely correct and appropriate expression.

We actually don't have control over a lot of our life, really. We don't really know how it's all going to turn out.

But there are many, many blessings right in front of our eyes.

And it is a pretty wonderful world, especially when you can let go of pre-conceptions of how it's supposed to be and just live with what is.

At least, that's how it works for me. And it has been a glorious lesson that I learned, as a gift, from being childless.

I'd like to end my essay with wishes:

If you are childless like me and in the middle of your journey, may you be filled with peace and joy in noticing the wonder of ALL that you never expected to create and receive.

If you are a mom, I hope you will look at a childless woman through different eyes. I hope you will look at her as someone who made a strong decision. I hope you will understand she may, in fact, love children as much as you do.

If you are reading this, with or without children, I hope you will try to suspend any sort of definition of what life is supposed to be. We are all doing the best we can.

And there is so much that is truly beautiful right here and now.

"Treasure this day, and treasure your self. Truly, neither will ever happen again."
Ray Bradbury

"There will come a time when you will believe everything is finished. That will be the beginning."
Louis L'Amour

www.ingramcontent.com/pod-product-compliance
Ingram Content Group UK Ltd.
Pitfield, Milton Keynes, MK11 3LW, UK
UKHW041958230426
12048UKWH00008B/409